Contents

Introduction

Watching birds in the garden has often been the starting point for many of us who have since gone on to enjoy a lifelong interest in birds, and in wildlife generally. One day, either at a young age or perhaps later in life, you will notice a bird in your garden. You become transfixed by its beauty, fascinated by what it is doing, or simply curious because you have never noticed it before. This can be the first step on a long and very enjoyable, journey!

A garden can be considered to be one's own personal little patch of countryside, and so the birds seen in it assume a special importance. Aside from the feeling of 'ownership', the ease of observation and the confiding nature of birds in this often intimate environment provide a perfect introduction to the avian world. Garden birds are usually watched from within the house, and because the observer is frequently hidden from their view, they generally behave in a more confiding fashion than is usual in the presence of people, and often at very close range. This is how many of us start watching birds, and even for those who have had the opportunity to go birding in exotic parts of the world, the birds in the garden of one's own home will always have a special quality that is difficult to match.

It does not matter where your garden is, or how large it is. You will still find birds to watch, even in the most urban of areas. As more than 80 per cent of people in Britain live in cities and towns, this is where many take their first steps into the wonderful world of watching birds. Wherever you are, this book is intended as a companion guide to help you get the most out of garden birding. The various sections are designed to help you become a better garden birdwatcher, from developing your recognition skills to creating new habitats for birds in your garden. There are detailed accounts for 17 different bird species, as well as advice on which plants are best for birds, what food to put out, and how to provide bird-friendly features such as ponds and nest boxes. While you can never be sure which birds will turn up in your garden and when, one thing is guaranteed – that watching birds will give you many hours of pleasure and that your own garden is one of the best places to start. Good luck!

TAWNY OWL
STRIX ALUCO

Garden Habitats and Environment

The habitats in your garden will largely determine which birds and other wildlife occur there. From the simplest urban plot to a lush verdant tangle of vegetation within a larger wilderness, you will be able to see birds. There is, however, a sliding scale of bird diversity that runs in tandem with the general biodiversity of your garden. The more attractive a garden is in terms of plants and invertebrates, the greater the number and variety of birds to be found there.

Birds require four basic components: food, water, shelter and nesting sites. If you want to see more birds in your garden, then you should consider taking steps to increase its attractiveness to them by providing more opportunities for these core essentials. The bird species found in your garden will vary according to the part of the country in which you live. While the species included in this book are meant to represent a reasonably comprehensive range of the birds likely to be encountered in a garden, some inner-city gardens will just not be large or diverse enough to attract more than the basic range of species. However, many people live in suburbs, where gardens are generally larger and the number of visiting bird species rises dramatically. Gardens located in a rural village or the open countryside, adjacent to areas of rich wildlife habitat or simply close to the coast, will attract even more species, including some that may well be in addition to those covered in this book.

- **Black-headed Gull**
- **Collared Dove**
- **Woodpigeon**
- **Feral Pigeon**
- **Swift**
- **Carrion Crow**
- **Magpie**
- **Starling**
- **Blackbird**
- **Wren**
- **Blue Tit**
- **Great Tit**
- **Robin**
- **Dunnock**
- **Greenfinch**
- **Chaffinch**
- **House Sparrow**

WREN
TROGLODYTES
TROGLODYTES

The following list of 17 species can be considered the 'base layer' of birds likely to be seen in, and from, a typical urban garden:

HOUSE MARTIN
DELICHON URBICA

Ponds

The simplest and most effective thing you can do to increase the diversity of wildlife in your garden is to install a pond. Even the smallest pond will attract invertebrates, amphibians and in turn birds, who will use it to drink and bathe. If you have just moved into a new home, or have yet to organize the garden space, then you may want to consider putting in a pond first, before you arrange the other features of the garden. Think carefully before you begin as, once in place, ponds are hard to move!

Ponds can be made quite easily, with the main work involved being the digging of the hole.

Pre-formed pond liners available in garden centres may be useful, but if you make your own hole then you have more control over the shape, design and depth. Ideally, a pond should have variable depths and at least one sloping edge, so that birds and animals can use the shallower slopes to bathe or to climb in and out.

Steep edges are no good for frogs and newts, which then need some kind of ramp in order to get in or out of the water. You will need some Butyl liner, which can be bought off the roll in many garden centres, and once you know how much space you can dedicate to your pond, you will need to calculate the amount of liner required. To do this, you need to work on (length + (deepest depth x2)) x (width + (depth x2)), and add 30–45cm to each figure for the overlap, which is essential for anchorage. Do not forget to make sure that there is enough liner to overlap the ground level edges. Any unsightly exposed liner can be covered by a roll of fresh turf. Old bits of carpet laid on the soil are useful in providing a barrier between any sharp stones and the liner. The depth of the pond is also quite important. You should make sure that it is at least 60cm in its deepest part, to prevent total freezing in winter.

If the pond is filled with tap water, it should be left for a couple of weeks before adding plants. The best way to fill a pond is with rainwater, and it can be collected via a rain diverter (available in garden centres), attached to a downpipe on the house. This can generate huge amounts of water, and it may be best to route it into a large water butt which can then overflow into the pond; the stored water can be used to top up the pond during dry spells.

A pond will take some time to mature, but you can help it along by adding plants. Make sure you only introduce native pond plants, best sourced from other pond-owning friends, a good garden will use it to drink and bathe. If you have just moved into a new home, or have yet to organize the garden space, then you may want to consider putting in a pond first, before you arrange the other features of the garden. Think carefully before you begin as, once in place, ponds are hard to move!

Ponds can be made quite easily, with the main work involved being the digging of the hole. Pre-formed pond liners available in garden centres may be useful, but if you make your own hole then you have more control over the shape, design and depth. Ideally, a pond should have variable depths and at least one sloping edge, so that birds and animals can use the shallower slopes to bathe or to climb in and out. Steep edges are no good for frogs and newts, which then need some kind of ramp in order to get in or out of the water. You will need some Butyl liner, which can be bought off the roll in many garden centres, and once you know how much space you can dedicate to your pond, you will need to calculate the amount of liner required.

To do this, you need to work on (length + (deepest depth x2)) x (width + (depth x2)), and add 30–45cm to each figure for the overlap, which is essential for anchorage. Do not forget to make sure that there is enough liner to overlap the ground level edges. Any unsightly exposed liner can be covered by a roll of fresh turf. Old bits of carpet laid on the soil are useful in providing a barrier between any sharp stones and the liner. The depth of the pond is also quite important. You should make sure that it is at least 60cm in its deepest part, to prevent total freezing in winter.

If the pond is filled with tap water, it should be left for a couple of weeks before adding plants. The best way to fill a pond is with rainwater, and it can be collected via a rain diverter (available in garden centres), attached to a downpipe on the house. This can generate huge amounts of water, and it may be best to route it into a large water butt which can then overflow into the pond; the stored water can be used to top up the pond during dry spells.

A pond will take some time to mature, but you can help it along by adding plants. Make sure you only introduce native pond plants, best sourced from other pond-owning friends, a good garden centre or a pond specialist. If you think you want fish in your pond, then it is a straight choice between fish and other wildlife, such as frogs and newts, as the

GREEN WOODPECKER JUVENILE
PICUS VIRIDIS

available, and the native flora will attract many insects, which in turn will benefit the birds.

The structure of your garden will also play a part in terms of the birds you will be able to attract. The tall growth of trees and shrubs may stand out as an island of greenery if surrounding gardens and spaces are without, and so will attract birds into the safe perches and potential breeding sites. Depending on the size of the garden, you may want to restrict the amount of growth in order to see more clearly what is going on, either from your vantage point within the house or as you sit out on a warm summer's afternoon. Wider open spaces may bring in larger birds, or allow ground-feeding species to feed undisturbed; for this they need a clear view all around, to allow them early warning of marauding predators, alongside proximity to cover to which they can retreat when danger looms.

Pests and Predators

It should be said first of all that one person's pest might be another person's cuddly countryside creature! However, the fact remains that birds are subject to a range of predators, natural and otherwise, and in the garden environment these can be artificially concentrated, sometimes reaching pest proportions and having a serious impact on bird populations and behaviour.

Grey Squirrels are a major pest in Britain, robbing birds' nests of eggs and young, and are thought to be responsible for the recent declines in species such as Spotted Flycatcher. They also cause damage to bird feeders by gnawing through plastic. An effective remedy is to buy squirrel-proof feeders to discourage them from visiting your garden.

Rats are also a nuisance, and will rob nests of eggs and young. They are attracted to bird seed spillage and to food scraps thrown on the ground, so beware of allowing your feeding stations to become too messy. Always wear gloves when handling your bird feeders, as rats can be vectors for disease.

Cats are incredibly damaging to wildlife. They are almost impossible to keep out of a garden, and frequently reach pest proportions in many suburban areas. It is estimated that cats kill 15 Robins for every one taken by a natural predator such as a Sparrowhawk. This is an awkward subject, on which emotions can run high. Cat-owners sometimes struggle to understand the impact that their pets are having on local bird populations, but at the same time one must acknowledge the great pleasure cats can give to their owners. Indeed, many bird-lovers are also cat-owners. Although the bottom line remains that cats will kill birds, there are various ways in which the level of destruction can be reduced.

SPOTTED FLYCATCHER JUVENILE
MUSCICAPA STRIATA

BLACKBIRD
TURDUS MERULA

On the basis that prevention is usually better than cure, keeping cats out of the garden in the first place is the best option, however difficult to achieve! One measure you can introduce, to try and frustrate their ingress, is to block corners and any gaps in the garden perimeter with branches cut from brambles and other spiky plants, and perhaps shield areas where birds come to feed with spiky palisades to hamper the progress of intruders. Hedging with Hawthorn or other densely growing shrubs can help, or you can attach obstacles to the tops of fences where cats jump over, such as expanding trellis strips laid lengthways. There are also some electronic repellent devices available, whereby a unit emits a signal that is disliked by cats. If elaborate palisades and access points are so arranged that the only way in for a cat is guarded by one of these, then they may be effective. However, there is evidence that cats will learn to adapt their routes around these devices, rather than be scared away completely.

Chasing away cats on foot can bring short-term success, but is rather labour-intensive and it can be difficult to maintain 24-hour coverage! The success of physical deterrents largely depends on hitting the target, and it should always be borne in mind that it is illegal to knowingly cause suffering to a cat. However, a water pistol will usually yield results, without harming the animal, and if used regularly, the cat may eventually react just to the sound of a window or door opening which usually precedes the attack, so that before long your garden could be largely free of cats during daylight hours. Failing that, get yourself a dog!

If cat presence in a garden is terminated suddenly, it is remarkable how quickly small birds will reappear. In cases where cats cannot be totally excluded from a garden, it is worth asking their owners to attach a small bell to their pet's collar. The noise of the bell, as the cat rushes forward towards its intended prey, gives birds a critical split second warning, which is often time enough for them to take flight. Evidence suggests that cats with bells on their collars catch up to 40 per cent fewer birds than those without.

Nest Boxes and Nesting

Nest boxes are a great way to study the lives, ecology and behaviour of birds in the garden, and over sixty different species have been recorded using them. Although next boxes vary considerably in terms of the precise arrangements required to attract particular species, they are usually simple wooden structures that can be homemade or bought from an ever-increasing array of retailers.

One issue that must be considered when thinking of erecting a nest box is how busy the garden is. During the breeding season birds are strongly territorial, and if a box is sited too near to feeding stations, then it is unlikely to be occupied – the stress of having to chase away so many visitors would be too much! A quiet place, at least five metres from any feeding point, would be satisfactory. It is also important to locate a nest box where it is secure from predators such as cats, rats and squirrels; open boxes definitely require a discreet and hidden location, as they are also at risk of predation by corvids. As Great Spotted Woodpeckers will attack nest boxes to take small chicks, hole-entrance boxes can be protected by fixing a metal plate with a hole of the same dimensions over the front of the box, preventing woodpeckers from enlarging the hole and reaching the young inside.

The classic bird nest box is a wooden structure with a sloping roof, and a round hole cut in the upper front plate. The diameter of the entrance hole will determine possible occupants:

25mm:	**Blue Tit, Coal Tit**
28mm:	**Great Tit, Tree Sparrow, House Sparrow**
32mm:	**House Sparrow, Nuthatch, Pied Flycatcher**
45mm:	**Starling**
50mm:	**Green, Greater and Lesser Spotted Woodpeckers**
150mm:	**Jackdaw, Stock Dove**

Robins, Wrens, Pied Wagtails and Spotted Flycatchers prefer a box with half the front panel open. Among the larger birds that will use nest boxes, Kestrels favour a square, open-fronted box, 150mm deep by 50mm wide, with an overhanging roof. Tawny and Barn Owls will use a box that is open on one side, with a base of 200mm square and sides 750mm high. They also like the box to be mounted under the shelter of eaves or a large branch, and angled at 45 degrees to the wall or branch. A special artificial nest can encourage House Martins and Swallows. Swifts will also use nest boxes designed specifically for them, but have to be lured in with sound recordings before they will inspect them. Further information about the many different types of nest box is available from the websites of bird protection societies such as the RSPB or BTO in the UK and increasingly from specialist bird feed suppliers.

It is important for a bird box to have a sloping and overlapping roof to divert excess rain, and drainage holes drilled through the floor panel to prevent waterlogging. For most species the box should be placed as high as possible on a wall or tree, well out of harm's way, but for smaller open-front box nesters, such as Robin and Wren, it needs to be located fairly low down (20–120cm off the ground) and partly or wholly hidden from general view. The box needs to open easily for cleaning at the end of each breeding season, an essential procedure for which a hinged roof should suffice. Be sure to remove any old nesting material and use boiling water to kill any remaining parasites and bugs, allowing the box to dry out thoroughly afterwards. Some nest boxes for small birds often have a removable upper half to the front plate, so you can choose or alternate between having a hole-entrance box or an open-fronted box. Taking care to ensure that they are securely fixed, boxes should always be placed on north- or east-facing walls or trees, thereby avoiding the hottest sun (from the south) and wet prevailing winds (largely from the west). Beware of cheaper boxes with thin walls – thicker walls provide better insulation against temperature extremes and rainfall.

Nest boxes should be erected no later than February, as any later than this and the birds may have already selected a nesting place. Boxes should also be left in place during the winter, as birds may use them as roosting places. Of course, not all the nest boxes in a garden will be used every year, and sometimes not by the species for which they are intended! I erected a 'House Sparrow terrace', a large box with three separate units, each with their own hole, as there are many House Sparrows in my area. I have never seen a House Sparrow even look at the box, but it is used successfully by Blue Tits and Great Tits in alternate years!

Providing nest material is also an option if you want to give birds further help. Hair, wool, feathers from old pillows, cotton and straw are all useful items, and these can either be scattered about or made available via a tidy, dedicated nest-material point, such as a piece of wire mesh attached to a tree trunk. If you have a large enough garden pond with muddy edges, House Martins can collect

Pied Flycatcher
FICEDULA HYPOLEUCA

their building materials here, and are more likely to nest on your house than if they have to find a mud source elsewhere.

Care should be taken during the breeding season not to disturb nest boxes or open the lids to look in and see if there are eggs or young. If you really want to see what is going on inside, it is possible to buy a unit with a small camera similar to a webcam, allowing the nest to be monitored from your computer or TV. These can be purchased from the websites of bird protection societies such as the RSPB in the UK.

Black-headed Gull
Larus ridibundus

Length: 34–37cm

Wingspan: 100–110cm

ADULT SUMMER PLUMAGE

The familiar small gull in our region. The adult in summer has a chocolate-brown (not black) head, and shows various transitional states between this and the winter plumage of a white head with just a dark smudge over the eye and a bold dark ear-spot. The upperparts are pearly grey, with a long white wedge from the primary coverts to the outer primary tips, a black trailing edge to the primaries and smoky grey underside to the flight feathers. Immature birds take two years to mature, and are blotched and marked with dark brown in decreasing amounts with age, but always have a roughly similar pattern of black and white on the primaries as the adult.

Common throughout our region and fairly ubiquitous in most wetland habitats. It breeds on a variety of open areas close to water, both coastally and inland, in a raucous colony that is unlikely to go unnoticed. Outside the breeding season Black-headed Gulls are found even more

WINTER PLUMAGE

widely, in urban areas, parks, playing fields, sewage farms, rubbish tips, reservoirs, inlets, estuaries and intertidal areas. They are a familiar sight around towns and villages, where they will cruise around, foraging and scavenging wherever they can find food, and often appearing from nowhere to swoop down on scraps (bread and chips seem to be particular favourites) thrown out by householders. They infrequently land in small enclosed areas, being nervous of places where their airspace is restricted, but are otherwise easy to lure in with food as they hover to pick up any suitable morsels, or even catch them in mid-air. They are noisy when coming to food, squabbling and screeching until the food is depleted, after which they quietly disperse.

Nesting occurs from April to July around shallow brackish and saline marshy pools, lakes, gravel pits, reedbeds, saltmarshes, estuaries, broad slow-moving rivers and flooded areas. Birds often favour small shingly islands for security but also use drier areas close to water, such as heather moors and dunes. The nest is a shallow scrape carelessly lined with vegetable matter, in which two to three eggs are laid and incubated by both sexes for 23–26 days. A short time after hatching the chicks leave the nest but remain in its vicinity, being tended by both parents until able to fly, which occurs after five or six weeks.

It is very vocal, particularly around breeding colonies where the noise can be deafening and often continues through the night. It has a variety of rather unattractive harsh calls, the commonest of which is a downwards-inflected screech "krreearr" or "kaa'aarrr". It also gives a harsher and insistent "raaargh!" or "gaaarhh!" when reacting anxiously to the presence of intruders. A softer and less urgent "aaarrrr", "akh'akh'akh", and singles and multiples of "kik", are all delivered in a more conversational tone. A longer and more elaborate call, "kre-kre-kreh'kraaa'kraaaa'kraaaa'kraaaa", is given in various social contexts.

1ST WINTER PLUMAGE

Rock Dove & Feral Pigeon
Columba livia

Length: 31–34cm

Wingspan: 63–70cm

The familiar 'town pigeon' has been with mankind for a very long time. Today's birds, with their highly variable plumage, are the descendants of wild Rock Doves, previously cultivated for food in large dovecotes or bred as racing pigeons. The original plumage of the Rock Dove is an attractive combination of greys; pale grey on the wing coverts and mantle, darker grey on the head, neck and breast, and with two bold black wingbars or 'straps' across the wings. It shows an iridescent green-and-purple patch on the side of its neck, and is distinct from other pigeons in having a white-rump (although some populations lack this); the tail is mid-grey with a narrow black terminal band. The underwing is white with a narrow black border, a feature that sets it apart from both the Woodpigeon and Stock Dove. It has a conspicuously fast and dashing flight, much more so than most of its relatives, and also wheels and glides effortlessly, being totally at home in the air.

Really wild Rock Doves have decreased drastically and are absent from England and Wales, with colonies persisting only in remote coastal regions of Scotland, Ireland and the

wildest corners of northern Europe, although how much mixing there has been of wild birds with their feral congeners is often hard to gauge. They are found around sea cliffs and in caves, gorges and on suitable rock faces in mountainous areas. Despite the famed homing abilities over long distances of racing pigeons, Rock Doves are usually sedentary. Feral Pigeons are often abundant in towns and cities, and are a common sight in the centre of urban areas, strutting about on pavements.

Feral Pigeons nest on the ledges of buildings and bridges high off the ground, as well as inside derelict buildings and in any niche that provides a suitable nesting space, so long as it is not too far from drinking water and bathing places. The display flight is not dissimilar to that of the Woodpigeon, with a

swooping flight accompanied by wing claps. The nest is made of a variable amount of local vegetation or litter, and breeding occurs from March to September. Two eggs are laid and incubated by both sexes for 16–19 days. The young are brooded continually at first, and fed by both parents. They can fly at five weeks.

This is a bird with a limited vocal repertoire and no contact calls or calls given in flight. The common and familiar 'hoo' calls are the territorial advertising calls of the male. He gives a rolling, moaning "u'u'u'uh'ohrwrrr" or a shorter 'uh'owrrr", also rendered as "ooohrrrr" or "ohh-oo-oor" and repeated several times. Females give a variant of this call that is hoarser and softer, and when a pair are together they give some more hurried and excited guttural sounds as part of their sexual attraction display.

Woodpigeon

Columba palumbus

Length: 40–42cm

Wingspan: 75–80cm

The largest of our pigeons, a very plump and heavy bird with a small head and medium-long tail. It is light blue-grey all over, with a prominent white patch on the side of the neck. The flight feathers are black and contrast with the grey wing coverts, which are bisected by a prominent white transverse bar on the upperwing which is mostly obscured at rest. The tail has a greyish-white subterminal band and a broad black terminal band. The deep chest is washed purplish-pink. Woodpigeons can appear rather long-necked, particularly when craning to reach seed feeders that are supposed to provide for sparrows and finches!

Very common and even abundant in many places, the population has undergone a steady and steep increase since at least the mid-1970s. They can be found in parks, gardens and urban areas, forests, small scattered or fragmented woodlands, and particularly in agricultural areas and fields where they often feed in huge flocks.

platform in a tree or bush, often flimsy enough for the eggs to be seen from below through the twigs. Two eggs are laid and incubated by both parents for 17 days, and following hatching the squabs are fed by both sexes and fledge after 33–34 days. Pigeons feed their young a 'milk' formed from sloughing off fluid-filled cells in the crop lining, which is apparently more nutritious than human or cow's milk. As a garden bird, they are a fairly universal, if not always popular, addition to the bird table, dominating and bullying through their sheer size and apparent clumsiness. Pigeons thrive on the wheat and other seeds contained within cheaper versions of mixed birdseed and which are thrown aside by small birds, which are more selective about what they eat.

British birds are resident, but large numbers of immigrants arrive for the winter from northern and eastern parts of Europe, and can be seen in large numbers at migration watchpoints. The spread of intensive arable cultivation (oilseed rape in particular) has been shown to promote winter survival rates, which may explain the rise in numbers. It has also been established that the Woodpigeon breeding season has advanced in response to the switch to autumn sowing, and thus earlier ripening, of cereals, with more pairs nesting in May and June and relatively fewer in July–September.

They nest almost anywhere, even in towns, the male bringing twigs for the female to fashion a

The commonly heard song is one of the classic sounds of the summer months, and is given from early spring through to autumn. It is a deep, five-syllable "wooh-oooo, wor-ooh, woh-WHOOR-ooh, wor-hoo, woh-WHOOR-ooh, wor-hoo, wu-WHOOR-ooh, wor-hoo", repeated three to five times, and often finished with a short upward-inflected "whu!" Another call is given by the male in a bowing display towards the female, a low growling "whu'-oorr", repeated at intervals. The familiar display flight consists of a short steep climb, at the apex of which the bird delivers several loud wing claps, before gliding back down. When disturbed, birds will make a lot of wing clapping and clattering noises on take-off, which functions as an alarm call.

Collared Dove

Streptopelia decaocto

Length: 31–33cm
Wingspan: 47–55cm

The Collared Dove is a relatively rare phenomenon – a bird that has naturally and emphatically colonized Britain. It is now common and even abundant in many areas, particularly in gardens, and their soft cooing has become part of the suburban soundscape.

In fact, before 1955 it had never even been recorded in this country, yet in that year it arrived at Cromer in Norfolk and started breeding, part of a remarkable expansion of its range in south-east Europe, from where the population spread northwestwards from the 1930s onwards. It has since colonized all of Britain up to Shetland, has reached the Faeroe Islands and even Iceland, and also now breeds quite far north in Scandinavia.

A medium-sized dove, it is much more slender and elegant than the Woodpigeon, weighing just 40 per cent of the most well-fed examples of that species. Overall it is a pallid greyish-buff mushroom colour, with a browner cast to the back and wings. It has an obvious black half-collar, a beady eye, grey flight feathers and a pale blue-grey panel on the greater coverts. The tail is quite long, with a broad white terminal band on all but the central feathers.

In western Europe, and indeed throughout much of its range, it is commonest in urban and suburban areas, utilizing habitats such as gardens,

both sexes for 16–17 days, and both parents feed the chicks until they leave the nest after 17–19 days. It can raise three broods a year, and sometimes as many as five.

A very vocal dove that sings throughout much of the year, yet its vocal range is limited. The commonly heard advertising call is a trisyllabic hollow cooing, with the first syllable a little higher in pitch and somewhat more emphatic, the second syllable also emphatic but the longest of the three notes in duration, the third syllable being shorter and rather 'swallowed', as in "Ooh'OOO-oo Ooh'OOO-oo Ooh'OOO-oo...". It has one other commonly heard call, a rather thin and nasal "eerrrrr" or "rrrrrehh", given in excitement, in flight and upon alighting. It also produces noisy wing flaps when flushed.

parks, churchyards and orchards, as well as farmyards. A seed-eater, it has benefited greatly from garden seed feeders, clearing up the grain that spills onto the ground below. It can be found wherever there are a few dense trees together with numerous perches such as telephone poles and wires. In the core of its range in India it is a bird of drier habitats, found even in semi-desert.

It builds a thin platform of a nest in a tree (or more rarely on a ledge), constructed of fine twigs and stems. Two eggs are laid and incubated by

Swift

Apus apus

Length: 16–17cm

Wingspan: 42–48cm

A remarkably well-adapted bird, leading an almost entirely aerial life. A true harbinger of summer, its arrival in the sky is a welcome and uplifting sign that warmer weather is on its way. It is remarkably regular in its arrival every year, always to within a few days, and it is a sad day when the flocks depart again (typically in mid-August, but with regional variations). Often confused with Swallows and House Martins by novices, the plumage, flight action, shape and voice of the Swift are all pointers for easy separation.

The plumage is uniformly dark brown, although often appearing black at range or in poor light, and with a whitish throat. It has a slender cigar-like body with a short forked tail, a short rounded head and very long and narrow sickle-shaped wings that are almost entirely 'hand', the 'elbow' or carpal joint lying very close to the body. Swifts have very small feet that are only designed for clinging to rock faces, and they never perch except to roost and when visiting the nest. They fly strongly, their narrow wings appearing to flicker in rapid flight, although for most of the time they glide or soar, even sleeping on the wing, which they achieve through shutting down one hemisphere of the brain at a time.

Swifts are found over virtually every habitat, the choice dictated only by the availability of flying insects. They can often be seen feeding low over water bodies in poor weather, conditions under which aquatic insects are more likely to emerge than terrestrial ones. They avoid large weather systems, leaving the area completely, but in fine weather use all available airspace and are a regular summer sight over most gardens.

Originally adapted to nesting in cliff crevices or even in cavities in trees, in modern times Swifts

have nested in urban areas, in older buildings, churches and houses, using roof eaves, spaces under dislodged tiles, wall cavities and any available crack or crevice. They have suffered in recent years from modern building techniques that exclude them from such nesting sites. The nest is made of windblown plant material that is collected in the air, and then glued together with saliva to make a shallow cup. Two or three eggs are laid from the end of May and are incubated for 18–20 days by both adults, although the eggs are adapted to withstand cooling and incubation periods can be longer. The young are fed by both parents, who bring a mass of insects packed into their visibly bulging throats. The chicks remain in the nest for 35–56 days and can withstand periods of hunger during bad weather by living off their fat reserves, although this extends the time spent inside the nest. They are fully independent once they fly the nest. Swifts can be lured to a nest site or a commercially

available swift nest box by the playing of recordings (which can be purchased on CD or downloaded free at www. commonswift.org) specially designed to attract them. They are sociable creatures and appear to thrive on nesting colonially; recordings can be played in the first weeks after their arrival from Africa, as well as later in the breeding season, when the previous year's young are prospecting for next year's nest sites.

During the breeding season Swifts are quite vocal, particularly in the evening, when nesting birds will perform a group screaming display, racing around their loose colony in a fast-moving flock, sometimes joined by other birds calling from within their nests. Non-breeders will also do this when gathering prior to ascending to higher altitudes for aerial roosting. The calls are high-pitched, shrill trilling sounds, varying in pitch and tempo, as in "rrrheeeiiii....", "ssrrriiii..", "zrrreeee.." or "iiiiirrrrrreeeeee..", sometimes begun more slowly with hoarse stuttering sounds.

Green Woodpecker
Picus viridis

Length: 31–33cm

Wingspan: 40–42cm

MALE

The second-largest woodpecker in Europe (after the mighty Black, not described here) and a brightly coloured bird with green upperparts and a fairly well-contrasting yellow-green rump, which is particularly noticeable in flight. The underparts are pale greenish-grey, and it has a long and powerful horn-coloured bill. The head and face are boldly marked, with a red crown that extends to the nape and a black face punctuated with a staring white eye. It has a short black moustache that is centred with red in the male but is all black in the female. The flight of all woodpeckers is very characteristic; as the tail is short and stiff, it cannot be used as a rudder when the bird is flying and the flight pattern therefore takes the form of deeply undulating bounds, with the wings held close in to the body every three or four wingbeats. Green Woodpeckers spend more time on the ground than any other woodpecker, with a distinctive and fairly upright carriage and the tail held low. Turf-dwelling ants are

JUVENILE

FEMALE

a favourite food, and it has a very long tongue with which to lick them up.

A familiar and common bird that is resident across our region. It avoids dense forest and is found in open broad-leaved woodlands with clearings, forest edge, large gardens, parkland, orchards, hedges with mature trees, farmland, rough grassland and heaths with scattered trees. It can often be encountered on the ground in areas with open ground, and especially on grassy areas such as lawns, golf courses and pastures. Green Woodpeckers are most likely to be encountered in larger suburban and rural gardens with mature deciduous trees and a lawn or grassy area for feeding. They are quite vocal, and can be heard particularly in the early morning, and also before and after rain. The nest hole is excavated by both sexes, in a mature tree with a fairly large circular or oval entrance hole leading to an unlined cavity that is 30–60cm deep. Nesting commences in April or May, when four to six eggs are laid and incubated by both

sexes for 19–20 days. After hatching, both parents feed the chicks a semi-liquid regurgitated mass, with fledging taking place after 21–24 days. Green Woodpeckers will occasionally use nest boxes.

The advertising call of the male, usually sung from high up in a large tree, is a far-carrying, slightly accelerating, laughing series of notes "hwa'hwa'hwa'hwa'hwa'hwa….", colloquially described as a 'yaffling'. It typically lasts for 1–3 seconds, dropping in pitch towards the end of the call and with a rate of about six 'yaffs' per second. The female gives a shorter, flatter 'yaffle', not dissimilar to the call of the Whimbrel. In flight both sexes give a loud, chuckling and often-repeated call of three or four syllables, as in "chyuk'chyuk'chyuk'chyuk" or "kye'kye'kye", also expressed when perched as an alarm or excitement call, and frequently given by young birds that are still accompanying their parents. The drum is rarely heard, but is said to be fairly quiet and 1.5 seconds in duration.

House Martin

Delichon urbica

Length: 13–15cm
Wingspan: 26–29cm

A familiar bird in suburban areas and villages, this is a dumpy and compact swallow with a simple and seemingly monochrome plumage pattern. It has blue-black upperparts, cap and tail, with a large white rump that serves as its most distinctive plumage character, easily seen in any view except for when the bird is directly overhead. The underside of the body and the underwing coverts are white, and the feet are feathered white, a visible feature when the bird is perched. The tail is rather short, but shows a prominent fork. The flight action is rather different to that of other swallows in our region, being slower with much gliding on straight wings, often in long lazy arcs, and it often flies high up when feeding. It perches freely on wires and on buildings, as well as on the ground when collecting mud for its nest. It is fairly sociable and gregarious, and large groups can be seen gathering on wires, especially after the young have fledged.

A summer visitor from Africa, typically present in northern Europe between April and October. Originally a cliff-nester, which is still the case in some parts of its range, it is now more commonly found around towns and villages. It avoids densely forested areas, and is less tied to water than some of its relatives. House Martins are frequently seen

with which to build its nest, so breeding sites will usually reflect the availability of a nearby source. The nest is made of mud pellets strengthened with plant fibres and lined with feathers, and takes both adults about 10 days to build. The nest is a deep and rounded half-cup, adhered to a vertical surface and with a small entrance at the top. Each nest contains roughly 1000 pellets of mud. Breeding occurs from May onwards, and four or five eggs are laid and incubated by both sexes for 13–19 days. The young are fed by both sexes and fledge after 19–25 days.

around gardens, owing to their choice of nesting habitat, and can be attracted to artificial nest boxes placed under the eaves of a house. They are easily seen over urban areas, hawking for insects high in the sky and often in the company of Swifts.

The nest is a closed mud-built structure, typically located under the eaves of houses but also on bridges and other man-made structures, and as a consequence it can be quite confiding of humans. Several nests are often built close together in a small colony, and it requires a good supply of mud

The commonly heard note is the contact call, a short dry stony rattle with a bright quality, as in "prrrt", either monosyllabic or often repeated two or three times in rapid succession, such as "jijitt", "prrrr-tit" and "jrrrr-tit'it". It also gives a shrill descending "schreeeo" as an anxiety call, often in response to aerial predators. All of these calls are typically heard from flying birds. The song is a made up of several call notes run together, plus a throaty rapid warbling, without any structured phrases, a rambling chuntering that is sung usually when close to the breeding area or at the nest itself.

Wren

Troglodytes troglodytes

Length: 9–10cm

Wingspan: 13–17cm

The Wren is one of the most abundant birds in Europe, with an estimated eight million territories in Britain alone, where it is resident throughout and found in a wide range of habitats. A tiny and restless little brown bird, with the distinctive habit of cocking its tail up and over its back, it is rather furtive and heard more often than it is seen. Frequently found skulking in dense undergrowth, it usually forages near to the ground and can be seen disappearing into crevices as it searches for invertebrates or flying between cover like a brown bee. The upperparts and head are a warm

reddish-brown, and the short wings are finely vermiculated and barred. The underparts are paler with mottling on the flanks. It has a slender bill and a distinctive long pale creamy supercilium.

A widespread and common bird throughout our region, particularly in woodland with dense undergrowth, also in scrub, hedges, gardens, parks, moorland where bracken-filled gullies offer shelter, sea cliffs and other rocky places with crevices, and occurring up to the treeline in some parts of its range. It is one of our more familiar garden birds, often nesting in a garden in almost any type of hole or cavity, even in unusual places in sheds, garages and other artificial structures. They roost communally in winter, cramming themselves into a nest or cavity, with their tails pointing outwards. The highest number of Wrens recorded at one such roost is an incredible 96!

Breeding commences in April, and the male Wren makes several nests of leaves, moss and grass; from these the female will select one that is to her liking and then line it with feathers. She will lay five or six eggs and incubate them alone for 16–18 days. Both parents feed the young, which fledge after 15–18 days. Although the species is single-brooded, the males are polygamous, sometimes having more than one female and accompanying nest at any one time, and staggering the timing so that they can help feed the young of each brood. Wrens easily desert their nest in the early stages of breeding, and care should therefore be taken not to disturb them.

Very vocal, with typical call notes being a hard "tchek" or "chudt", often extended into "tchek'eck'eck".

It also gives a low rattling churr. When anxious, near the nest or young, or in response to danger such as a cat, it gives a higher-pitched hard rattle, not unlike someone sucking on the corner of their mouth to produce a rasping sound, as in "tr'tr'tr'tr'tr'tr'tr". The song is remarkably loud and shrill for such a tiny bird, and is a very rapid series of well-structured piercing notes, usually including or ending with a loud trill. It usually lasts for 4–7 seconds, during which time it produces about 6–8 notes per second, such as "see'se'seow'see'seee'ch'ch'ch'ch'ch'see'suwi's uwi'see'su'ee'trrrrrrrrrr chu'chu'see!".

Dunnock

Prunella modularis

Length: 13–14.5cm
Wingspan: 19–21cm

A demure little bird that is frequently seen in gardens, although often skulking and unobtrusive, and usually seen shuffling, mouse-like, on the ground. Brown and grey, with a warm brown mantle clearly streaked with black, and dull grey-brown underparts with mottled brown streaks along the flanks. The head, neck, throat and breast are a clean lead-grey, with brown cheeks and a darker mottled crown. The bill is thin, black and warbler-like, and the legs are orange. Juveniles are plain brown, streaked and blotched with black, and with a whitish throat.

A familiar resident garden bird in Britain, and found anywhere with dense scrubby undergrowth. It is commonly encountered in gardens, parks, churchyards, open mixed woodland, farms, scrub, hedges, young conifer plantations, heaths and overgrown rough ground in urban areas, such as railway embankments, especially where it is a

DISPLAYING MALE

JUVENILE

little damp. It is attached to spruce forest in the northern parts of its range, where it is usually just a summer visitor. Primarily insectivorous, it does not use seed or nut feeders but in winter will eat small pieces of nut, seed kernels or nyger seed, taken from the ground.

Despite being something of a 'boring brown bird', it has rather exotic and complex breeding arrangements. Dunnocks are polyandrous, meaning that the female has two males in attendance, although this can extend to three females and three males, all in overlapping relationships! A typical scenario is where two males will sing and defend a territory for a single female, with both males courting her for sexual favours. The display of the male involves an eye-catching alternate wing-flicking, which serves to attract a female. A male intent on mating may be seen to peck around the cloaca of the female, to trigger an expulsion of sperm from another male that she has recently mated with. DNA studies of chicks have found that within a single brood there may be two fathers contributing. The nest is a stout cup of twigs and moss, lined with hair, wool or fine moss and built within a dense bush or hedge. Breeding commences in April, with four or five eggs being laid and incubated by the female for 14–15 days. The young are fed by both (or all!) parents, fledging after 12–15 days. There are two and sometimes three, broods.

The common call is a rather coarse, high-pitched "tiih", often repeated a number of times and made as both a contact call and as an alarm. It also utters a thinner, less coarse "seep", and a shivering "itititi", which is typically given outside the breeding season and is rather like the alarm call but more silvery in quality. The song is a high-pitched and scratchy little ditty, fairly rapid and expressed on a level tone without trills or flourishes, confusable with the song of the Wren but slower and much less emphatic, lasting between 1.5–3 seconds but also delivered in longer phrases. It is rather regular and unvarying, as in "ss'tsi'ti'si'ti'teew'ti'ti'deuw'tii'si'si'ti".

Robin

Erithacus rubecula

Length: 12.5–14cm
Wingspan: 20–22cm

A familiar garden bird for many, this is a delicate but plump bird, with brown upperparts and crown, a narrow buff wingbar, and a large orange-red breast extending across the face and over the bill, rimmed with a blue-grey border. The underparts are whitish with a brown wash on the flanks. Juvenile birds have the familiar rotund shape but are brown above with buff spotting, while the underparts are buff with dark spotting on the breast. They assume the adult-type plumage fairly quickly, gradually acquiring the patches of tangerine on the breast. Ground feeders, Robins hop along and pause watchfully, with flicks of the wings and tail. They are famously aggressive towards other Robins that stray within their territory, sometimes attacking the intruder in such a frenzy that it is blinded or even killed.

Essentially a forest bird, found in shady woodland with undergrowth, it is also commonly seen in gardens, parks and other managed places offering dense cover. In Britain it is a widespread resident and notably confiding, although in northern Europe it is migratory, frequents coniferous forest, and is much more retiring. The Robin is one of the most familiar British garden birds, notably tame when any digging is going on in the garden. It will perch nearby to take worms or other invertebrates unearthed by the gardener, a variation of natural behaviour in which it might follow Wild Boar in close attendance as they churn up the ground. Robins will visit feeders and bird

tables, and have a special liking for live food such as mealworms. As terrestrial feeders, they are very vulnerable to domestic cats. It has been estimated that cats kill 15 Robins for every one killed by natural predators such as Sparrowhawks.

Robins choose a wide variety of sites for nest-building, with any form of depression or hole considered. The nest is well hidden, and built by the female of moss, leaves and grass, with a lining of finer grass, hair and feathers. It can be located from ground level up to about 3m high, in a crevice or a sheltered bank, and sometimes in more unusual sites in the garden, such as discarded kettles, watering cans, flower pots, etc, and they can be attracted to nest in an open-fronted nest box. Breeding commences in March or April, with the four or five eggs incubated by the female alone for 14–16 days. After hatching, the female broods the chicks closely at first, with the male bringing food to all, after which both parents continue to tend the young until they fledge at 13–16 days. There are usually two and sometimes three broods in a year. The chicks are distinctive in having black down, and are able to merge into the shadows

when they lie prone, well camouflaged in the shady hollow of their nest.

Really quite vocal, a commonly heard call being a territorial note "tic", usually repeated as "tic-tic'tic", "pt-pt'pt" or often as "tikatik-tik", sometimes likened to the sound of an old-fashioned watch being wound up. It has a thin sharp "tseeeh", used in alarm. The song is heard throughout much of the year and frequently in autumn and winter, when resident local birds react territorially to the arrival of wintering birds from the Continent, and are often encountered singing at night around streetlights. It is a languid, melodic sequence of clear fluty whistles and rippling notes, switching between high and low frequencies and interspersed with pauses. Very variable, it typically commences with a few thin high notes, then drops into lower richer notes, often speeding up into a warbling trill and frequently including a "dee-diddlee'dee" phrase. Robins can sing at length, but phrases typically last for between 2–3 seconds, with measured pauses between.

Blackbird

Turdus merula

Length: 24–25cm
Wingspan: 34–38.5cm

JUVENILE

One of the most familiar garden birds, the Blackbird is very common and widespread and occurs in gardens in urban, suburban and rural areas. Its rich song is frequently heard as the males pronounce their territories from rooftops, aerials and garden trees, and their loud calls echo around the lanes and streets as dusk falls.

A strong-legged and sprightly ground-feeding bird, with a fairly long and broad tail. The male is uniformly black, with a bold orange-yellow bill and eye-ring. The female is almost completely dark brown, with a slightly paler central throat, faint mottling on the malar stripe and breast, blotched or spotted darker to a varying degree on the upper breast. The bill is usually brown and dull, with varying degrees of yellow-ochre showing through, with a dull yellow eye-ring. Recently-fledged juveniles have rufous tips to their body feathers, giving them a gingery appearance, while older immature birds are brown like the females, with a blackish-brown bill, the males in their first year showing a black tail and sooty plumage before acquiring their adult plumage. There are many documented cases of albinism, and it is not unusual to see Blackbirds with at least partially white plumage.

Blackbirds can be found in all types of forest and woodland with undergrowth, in farmland, scrub, copses, hedges, gardens and parks, as well as on moorland and in wetlands, provided that cover and undergrowth are available. Resident in Britain, its populations are supplemented in winter by northern and eastern birds migrating to western Europe. It often feeds on the ground under the cover of bushes and trees, where it turns over the leaf litter in search of food. Gardens provide a perfect habitat for the Blackbird, with grassy lawns offering feeding opportunities as it hunts for earthworms and insects. It will also take seeds and fruit, regularly coming to bird tables and to food scattered in open areas, although always favouring the proximity of cover to which it can retreat.

MALE

Gardens provide optimum nesting areas, with any dense bushy shrubs or trees favoured, also occasionally in a wall or building, anywhere from 1–10m off the ground and fairly well hidden. The female builds a rather large and deep nest in a fork, constructed of grass, roots, twigs etc, with a lining of mud and then a softer inner lining of finer materials. Breeding typically starts in March and April, and in a good year it can be double- or triple-brooded. The female typically lays three or four eggs, and does all the 13–14 days of incubation. The male assists in the feeding of the fledglings, which leave the nest after 14–16 days. Both adults feed the ginger-spotted youngsters for three weeks thereafter.

Blackbirds are rather vocal, their rich repertoire of calls making up a significant part of the soundscape of bird sounds around a typical garden. One of the loudest and therefore most familiar

MALE

FEMALE

is the alarm call, a loud, often hysterical, tinking and clucking, as in "chink chink chink chink…" or "plih! plih! plih!", when the neighbourhood birds start 'kicking off' at dusk prior to roosting, often accelerating the calls into a manic crescendo when a bird takes flight. This call is also used in mobbing situations, and may lead the observer to find an owl roosting in the daytime. Variations include a less intense, low "chuck chuck chuck". Another more subtle but commonly heard alarm call is the 'ground predator alert' call, commonly used for cats, which is a soft "pock" or "puhc", and frequently heard when parents have fledged young and are keeping watch for danger. It also has a thin and drawn-out, descending "sseeh", given in alarm, and a more rolling "srrri", typically used on migration. The song is rich, confidently languid and pleasing, with a series of fairly low-pitched fluty notes uttered in phrases lasting 2–4 seconds, usually tailing off into low chuckling notes and often with an equal length pause between. Each male has wide variety of song phrases, sung from a prominent perch such as a roof or treetop.

FEMALE

Long-tailed Tit

Aegithalos caudatus

Length: 13–15cm (inc. tail of 7–9cm)
Wingspan: 16–19cm

A cute little 'lollipop' of a bird, with a small body and very long tail. Round-headed, and with a tiny black bill, it is often seen moving in restless flocks with a weak bouncing flight, playing follow-my-leader across gaps in trees and along hedgerows. The head and underparts are whitish with a broad black band that runs from in front of the eye along the side of the crown to the nape, and faint black streaks on the cheek. The upperparts are black, with a large panel of dirty pink on the scapulars. The tail is black with white on the outer feathers, and the short stubby wings have broad white edges on the tertials and secondaries. Juveniles are browner than the adults, with more extensive dark markings on the head, and the pink areas of plumage are whiter. Northern populations of the nominate race have a completely snowy-white head.

The Long-tailed Tit is resident and found rather commonly across Britain, however northern populations occasionally undergo irruptions southwards. It favours deciduous and mixed woodland, with plenty of thick undergrowth such as hazel and willow, and is also found in scrub and bushy areas away from woodland, such as in gardens, parks, hedges in farmland and other marginal habitats with secondary growth. Frequently found in small flocks that keep together with constant contact calls, they can be quite fearless and inquisitive. These groups are often family parties, and birds can be seen zipping back and forwards, trying to keep together if one or more members of the party drop out of line. They occur often in gardens, travelling through in active feeding flocks, or even nesting within undisturbed corners. They are

strongly insectivorous, but will visit feeders to take advantage of fat cakes, seed mixes and peanuts.

The nest is an oval, domed structure built from moss and bound together with spider webs, coated with lichen on the outside and lined with feathers. It is usually placed in a fork in a dense or thorny bush, and is built by both adults. Breeding commences in April, and six to eight eggs are laid, with the female doing the majority of the incubation for 15–18 days, the male bringing food to her. Both parents feed the young, but occasionally they will have 'helpers' assisting the feeding, possibly involving related individuals whose own nest has failed. Fledging occurs after 16–17 days.

A noisy and vocal bird, frequently heard uttering a thin and weak-sounding "ssi'ssi'ssi'ssi" when in flight or as a contact note. This call is easy to mimic and they often respond by coming very close to the observer to investigate. Another commonly heard call is a dry and slurred "trrrr", and short little conversational "pt" note. It also gives a harder scolding "tsrr'r'r'r'r" when excited or alarmed, and an agitated and alert-sounding "tsrrr-tsrrr". Infrequently heard, the

song is a rather random and hurried collection of short, dry chipping notes, interspersed with nasal twittering and bubbling sounds and a few short melodious whistles.

JUVENILES

Blue Tit

Cyanistes caeruleus

Length: 10.5–12cm
Wingspan: 17.5–20cm

One of the most common and familiar garden birds, the Blue Tit is very small and lightweight with primrose-yellow underparts. It has a rounded head patterned with broad white cheeks, a white forehead and white extending in a ring around

JUVENILE

to the nape, isolating a rounded crown patch of blue. It has a blackish bridle through the eye, separating cheek from crown, and a darker blue collar-ring below the cheek, broadest at the rear and joining a blackish-blue chin and throat at the front. The mantle is green, and the wings and tail are blue with white tertial tips and a white wingbar on the tips of the greater coverts. Females are duller than males, and they are thought to select those partners that have the brightest caps, which glow brightly when seen in the ultra-violet spectrum. Juveniles are greenish-brown on the upper-parts and have yellow cheeks.

A common resident, it favours deciduous or mixed woodland and forest, parks, gardens, orchards, hedges, scrub, and indeed any bushy areas with scattered trees, wherever it can find a ready food supply and holes to nest in. It is a familiar visitor to garden bird feeders, especially in the winter months, when it also readily joins roaming mixed flocks.

Breeding commences in April, and both sexes build a nest of moss and hair inside the selected cavity. An average of 8–10 eggs are then laid and incubated by the female for 13–15 days, while the male brings food to her. The chicks are tended by both adults and fledge after 18–21 days, and follow the parents for some time after leaving the nest. Usually there is just one brood. Blue Tit broods are vulnerable to being 'cleaned-out' by various predators such as Grey Squirrels and Great Spotted Woodpeckers.

A commonly used call is a churring note, which starts low and rises in a short rolling trill, and is delivered in various permutations, such as "chwrrr'r'r'r'r'r", "chwrr'hi'ih'ih" or "twr'r'r'i'i'i'i'i", or commencing with high notes before dropping sharply, as in "tsii'tsii'tsii-chwrr'r'r'r'r". It uses a more scolding "trrrrr-bii'beep!" and a drawn-out "seeer" in response to aerial predators, a conversational high-pitched "tsee" when in a group, and a repeated drier note, "di'di'di'di". Song variants include a repeated high-pitched, clear silvery "bii'bi-sisisi-srr'r'r'r'r'r'r'r, bii'bi-sisisi-srr'r'r'r'r'r'r'r, bii'bi-sisisi-srr'r'r'r'r'r'r'r" and a high, cyclical and buzzing "tsee-zzi'zi, tzii'zi'zee- tzii'zi'zee- tzii'zi'zee- tzii'zi'zee".

During the breeding season it will feed on insects and caterpillars, and is an important species in the control of garden pests such as aphids. It is famous for its ability to learn how to open foil-capped milk bottles, to get at the cream in the top of the bottle, but this habit is seen much less these days with the reduction in doorstep deliveries and rise in the popularity of low-fat milk. It readily occupies nest boxes and can be further encouraged to take up residence in gardens by the provision of these; otherwise it can use any kind of hole, either natural or in some artificial structure.

Great Tit

Parus major

Length: 13.5–15cm
Wingspan: 22.5–25.5cm

The largest tit in the region and a very familiar garden bird, the Great Tit has an ebullient nature and striking plumage. The underparts are bright yellow, bisected by a bold black stripe running from throat to vent. The belly stripe on a male Great Tit is an indicator of his status, and females are attracted to males with bigger stripes. The head and throat are glossy black with a large white cheek patch that is fully enclosed. The mantle is green, and the wings are slaty-blue with a broad white wingbar on the tips of the greater coverts. The tail is quite long, grey-blue and with white outer feathers. Females are slightly less bright than the males and have a narrower black belly stripe; juveniles appear duller and washed out, with yellowish cheeks and a brown cap.

A common resident, it is found in similar habitats to the Blue Tit, such as deciduous and mixed woodland, sometimes in coniferous forest, plus hedges, thickets, parks, churchyards, gardens and virtually any area with scattered trees, shrubs and bushes. It is primarily a lowland bird, although it can occur up to the treeline in mountainous areas. It adapts well to the presence of man and is a regular visitor to bird feeders. It is insectivorous during the breeding season, preferring to feed its young on protein-rich caterpillars, and studies have shown that Great Tits have a significant impact in reducing

tii-twerr". It commonly utters a low purring or scolding, slightly rising "tchr'r'r'r'r'r", which can be combined with higher-pitched calls such as "tii'tii'wrrrrr". The song is also highly variable, but typically is a repeated series of two or three loud, clear and ringing notes repeated in a 'see-sawing' style for 3–10 times, though often just four or five. Studies have identified that Great Tits with the broadest repertoire of songs will be more successful in defending their territories, which is why they use so many different variations. These are just some of the many possible examples: "dti'too dti'too dti'too dti'too dti'too", "pu'tingk pu'tingk pu'tingk pu'tingk", "chi'wer chi'wer chi'wer chi'wer chi'wer", "ba'ba'ding-ba'ba'ding-ba'ba'ding-ba'ba'ding", and the classic "tea'cher tea'cher tea'cher tea'cher".

caterpillar damage in apple orchards. In autumn they will eat fruit, and in winter they switch to nuts and seeds. Like the Blue Tit, they have the ability to break the foil caps of milk bottles to plunder the cream floating on top.

The nest is in a hole of some kind, either natural or in an artificial structure (it readily uses nest boxes), and is built by the female of moss, roots, grass and spider webs, lined with down and feathers. Breeding commences in April and seven to nine eggs are laid. The female incubates for 13–15 days, while the male brings food to her. The chicks fledge after 18–21 days, and continue to be fed by the parents for another couple of weeks.

The Great Tit is highly vocal, with many different calls, often with a clear ringing bell-like quality. Variants include a "psi! ping ping", a Chaffinch-like "pink-pink", and a "tii-twerr,

Magpie

Pica pica

Length: 40–51cm (inc. tail of 20–30cm)
Wingspan: 52–60cm

This noisy character is familiar to many, with its distinctively pied plumage and long tail. The tail is glossed green and exceeds the length of the body, and males have longer tails than females. The head, breast, vent and upperparts are black, the belly white, and it has a long white stripe along the scapulars. The wings are black with a blue gloss and a large white panel across the whole of the primaries. The metallic sheen on the wings and tail varies between green, blue and purple, depending on the angle of the light. The flight is rather flappy, fluttering and direct. Juveniles are similar to adults, but sooty-headed, shorter tailed and less glossy.

The Magpie is a common and widespread resident found in a wide range of habitats. They are very adaptable, which has enabled them to colonize many new urban and suburban localities since the 1960s, although apparently this population 'surge' has now stabilized. It generally favours lightly wooded open country, with adequate open ground and short grass for feeding, and can be found in open deciduous and coniferous woodland, farmland with hedges, and often occurs close to man in villages, parks and gardens.

Its diet comprises largely insects (especially beetles), worms and other invertebrates, as well as fruit, seeds, carrion, food scraps and occasionally small vertebrates. It is often seen

MAGPIES AND
STARLINGS
SCAVENGING

plundering the nests of small birds of their eggs or young, but generally only does this when feeding its own offspring. In winter Magpies become very gregarious, feeding in flocks of variable size, and also gathering at communal roosts in the evenings. These flocks break up in spring when birds begin their breeding.

Magpie pairs are monogamous, mating for life, and begin breeding each April, when they build a ragged nest of sticks strengthened with mud, lined with softer plant material and with a roughly built dome of twigs over the top. Five or six eggs are laid, and the female incubates for 17–20 days. Both parents take part in feeding the young, which fledge after 26–31 days. A strong trend towards earlier laying has been identified and may be partly explained by recent climate change.

It has a range of calls, all rather harsh and unmusical, with the familiar 'rattle' call frequently heard. It is a "cha" or "jakh" note, rapidly repeated to make a staccato chattering, as in "jakh'akh'akh'akh'akh'akh", and is typically given in alarm or anxiety, such as when mobbing predators. Another commonly heard call is a two-note "ch'chack", "akh'jack" or "schrach-ak", and a single, more drawn-out "shree'akh", which are used in a conversational context and often heard when a group of birds are together. It has other, less well-defined harsh notes, and also a rarely heard song, used in courtship, which is a subdued chuntering and twittering interspersed with some sweet notes.

Jackdaw

Corvus monedula

Length: 30–34cm
Wingspan: 67–74cm

An amiable and gregarious small blackish crow, the Jackdaw is often seen in tight flocks in farmland and frequently mixed with Rooks. At range it can appear all dark, but with a reasonable view it shows a pale light-blue eye and a grey nape and sides to the head, contrasting with the charcoal-grey upperparts and black face, crown and throat. The underparts and remainder of the plumage are dark grey, and it has a rather short and slender bill. The nominate race or 'Nordic' Jackdaw, which breeds in Scandinavia,

NOMINATE RACE

has slightly paler and more mottled underparts, as well as a clearly defined silver collar at the lower edge of the neck sides. Juveniles are duller-plumaged and less contrasting.

Resident throughout our region, although northern birds wander southwards in autumn and winter. It is often found close to man, using chimneys and other cavities in buildings for nesting, and otherwise occurs in many types of open habitat with scattered trees. It often favours deciduous woodland where old hollow or mature trees with cavities are available, such as in old parkland and large gardens, and also occurs in

BRITISH RACE

farmland with mature hedgerows and locally in mountainous or cliff habitats and quarries. It feeds mostly on the ground, but also in trees. Its diet includes insects and other invertebrates, seeds, food scraps, shoreline fish carrion, animal feeds (particularly around outdoor-reared pigs), and it is more likely to take food from bird tables than other *Corvus* species. Jackdaws can often be seen together in pairs, being attentive to each other or flying around in tandem, as the male watches his female to make sure the offspring are all his own!

The nest is made within a large cavity, often in the chimney of a house or in the porous roof of an old building such as a church. It commonly nests in a large hole in a dead tree, and will use nest boxes with a large interior. Breeding commences in March and April, and both sexes take part in building the nest with a variable amount of twigs, depending on the size of the cavity. Nest territories are very small, so Jackdaws can often live in loose colonies. The female incubates the four or five eggs for 18–20 days, and both sexes feed the young. The fledglings leave the nest after 30–33 days.

A vocal bird, so much so that it is named after its commonly heard call, a rather high, bright and pleasing "tjakk!", "khakk" or "kyak", often repeated in a series or given in chorus by a flock, when it can sound like "k'chak k'chik k'chakk", or an even faster 'yickering' sound, such as when gathering to roost. It gives this or similar calls at varying volumes and intensities, such as quieter conversational 'chakking' from pairs sitting together, or when adults announce their return to the nest. It gives more of a crow-like 'caw' in alarm, a harsh drawn-out "jaairrr" or "kyarrrr". It also has a song, a quiet medley of call notes run together.

Carrion Crow & Hooded Crow

*Corvus corone &
Corvus cornix*

Length: 44–51cm

Wingspan: 93–104cm

CARRION
CROW

The Carrion Crow is the familiar all-black corvid over much of Britain and western Europe, with the similar Hooded Crow replacing it across Ireland, Scotland, Scandinavia and eastern Europe. They are both so similar in morphology and habits that they were considered by most authorities to be just geographical races of one species, as a limited amount of hybridization occurs where ranges overlap. Since 2002, however, the Hooded Crow has been elevated to full species status. The Carrion Crow has a slight metallic sheen to its plumage, but is otherwise uniform in colour.

Similar to the Common Raven, it can told apart by its smaller size, rounded tail, shorter bill, shorter wings and weaker flight, plus clear vocal differences. It is almost impossible to separate from a juvenile Rook, however, but shows a blunter, thicker bill. Generally less gregarious than the Rook, and also a solitary nester, it can however

HOODED
CROW

**CARRION CROWS MOBBING
LESSER BLACK-BACKED GULL**

carrion and scraps, and will kill and eat any small animal they can catch. They will also steal eggs and young chicks.

Breeding commences in April, and both species build a ragged nest of sticks and twigs, usually in a tree or bush and bound together with earth and lined with hair and wool. Three or four eggs are laid, and the female incubates for 18–20 days.

Both sexes feed the young, which fledge after 29–30 days. It is not uncommon for a youngster from the previous year's offspring to help rear the new hatchlings. Instead of seeking out a mate, it stays around its parents, looking for food and assisting with the feeding of the new young.

The calls of the Hooded and Carrion Crows are very similar. They are quite vocal, the

form flocks, particularly after breeding. The Hooded Crow is a pale dirty-grey on the body, with black wings and a black hood and breast.

Found commonly in a wide variety of habitats, they favour open country with scattered trees, woodland, parks and farmland with hedgerows, but commonly penetrate into urban areas, their only real habitat requirement being for trees in which to nest. Scavengers by nature, they will take advantage of human-inhabited areas in order to feed on the abundant waste. In Britain they can also be found foraging in tidal habitats, such as estuaries, saltmarshes and coastal areas, and Hooded Crows have a liking for bog habitats. They feed on invertebrates and cereal grain,

commonly heard call throughout the year being a repeated, slightly nasal "kraaaah" or a softer "oarrgh", which dip in pitch at the end of the note, with a slightly rolling and liquid tone at times and often repeated in a sequence of 2–6 notes. This call can be of varying pitch, and is sometimes delivered more urgently on a level tone, such as "kraaaa! kraaah!" or "kruaah-kruaah". The female can give a more mechanical-sounding "krrgh krrgh krrgh", reminiscent of a Raven's call but usually accompanied by the main call to avert any confusion. Hoarse and strangled-sounding variants may also be heard sometimes, and a rarely heard song of subdued variable notes is also given.

Starling

Sturnus vulgaris

Length: 19–22cm

Wingspan: 37–42cm

JUVENILES

Most people are familiar with this ubiquitous bird. It has a metallic green and violet sheen to its black plumage, a short tail and pointed triangular wings. In winter it is profusely spotted with buffish-white spots and has a dark bill, but in summer loses most of the pale spotting and appears wholly glossy black. The bill also turns yellow, with a blue-grey bill base in the male and a yellowish-white one in the female. Juveniles are a mousy grey-brown with a pale throat, gradually acquiring white-spotted black feathers during their first winter.

Resident in Britain and western Europe, with large influxes of birds in winter from further north and east, it is common and found in many different habitats, and is particularly attracted to urban areas. In recent years Starling numbers have declined, possibly attributable to pesticides killing the food on which their young depend. It can be found in woodland, farmland, on seashores, and indeed in almost any open country. Outside the breeding season it is highly gregarious, dispersing widely and sometimes forming massive flocks over roosting sites in the evening, providing a spectacular sight and sound. They fly in a tight spherical formation, frequently expanding, contracting and changing shape, seemingly without any leader. Larger roosts can cause problems through guano pollution killing the trees in which they roost. They forage on the ground, taking fruit, seeds and insects, typically amongst short-cropped grass, and can often be seen around (and sometimes on top of) grazing animals. In gardens they voraciously devour any food left out, and are very fond of fat balls. They will readily use nest boxes, provided the entrance hole is large enough.

Breeding commences in April, and unpaired males build a nest in any kind of hole to attract an unpaired female. The males often decorate nests with flowers and fresh greenery, which the female

WINTER
PLUMAGE

given in alarm when an aerial predator is about, and often a good indication of a Sparrowhawk in the area. The song is a rambling, continuous collection of rather strangled and subdued sounds, throaty warbling and musical whistles, many of them high-pitched, including much mimicry and unusual noises, such as a rising "schweee'errrr" and a descending "wheeeeeoooooooo" 'bomb-drop' whistle, plus clicking, gurgling and croaking noises, and scrunching sounds like a handful of ball-bearings being rubbed together. Starlings are famous for mimicking mechanical sounds such as telephones and car alarms!

SUMMER PLUMAGE

removes when she moves in and rebuilds it. The nest is typically constructed of straw, dry grass and twigs, and lined with feathers, wool, leaves and insect-repelling herbs. Four to five eggs are laid and incubated by both sexes for 12–15 days. The young are fed by both sexes and fledge after 19–22 days.

Starlings are very vocal, with a rich repertoire of song and mimicry. Commonly heard calls include a rasping descending "tchaaeerr", often given when taking flight. Other calls include a sharp repeated "kyik" or "kyett",

House Sparrow

Passer domesticus

Length: 14–16cm

Wingspan: 21–25.5cm

In spite of recent declines in some areas, the House Sparrow was still estimated to be Britain's most common garden bird as recently as 2006. It is a stout, large-headed and thick-billed bird, the male having a grey crown with a chestnut brown nape and head sides between crown and cheek, pale grey cheeks and greyish underparts. It has black lores, chin and throat, and a black upper breast that flares out into a broader patch. The mantle is brown and boldly streaked black, with a grey rump in summer. In winter it is duller and browner overall, with a reduced amount of black on the underparts. The female is more demure, grey-brown all over, heavily streaked on the mantle, and with a buff supercilium.

The House Sparrow is commonly found wherever there is human habitation, although in parts of urban Britain there has been a marked decrease in recent years. It ranges from city centres to small villages and particularly farms, and can be found feeding on farmland, especially in grain crops and typically where there

MALE

are hedgerows and other cover to which it can retreat. It generally avoids exposed, open spaces and densely vegetated or forested areas. House Sparrows are gregarious, nesting colonially and and gathering in communal roosts. Between August and October many colonies are abandoned as birds move onto arable land to take advantage of the temporary abundance of grain. Once the flocks break up in October, nesting colonies are reoccupied. They are aggressive birds, tending to dominate seed feeders in gardens and thereby preventing other birds from getting to the food. They adore black sunflower seeds and sunflower hearts, and close scrutiny of sparrows at feeders filled with cheaper mixed seed will reveal that they throw a lot of unwanted seed on the ground, as they try to get to their choice morsel!

They nest in loose colonies of up to 10–20 pairs, and since they do not defend a proper territory, nests can be as little as 20–30cm apart. Nests are located in crevices, holes and under loose roof tiles in buildings or, more traditionally, in a bush or a hole in a sandbank. Breeding commences in May or earlier, with four or five eggs being laid in a hole or crevice, in a cup-shaped (or sometimes a domed) nest built by both sexes, of grass and straw with a feather lining. The female does the majority of the incubation, which only lasts for 11–14 days. The parents share nesting duties equally, and the young are fed on aphids, caterpillars, weevils and grasshoppers, but seed and grain are the most

important foods by the time they fledge. Fledging occurs 14–16 days after hatching, and the young continue to be fed by the parents for 14 days, or by just the male when the female has already started incubating another brood. They have three broods in a year, and occasionally four. Pairs are faithful to each other for life.

A rather uncomplicated set of vocalizations that sound bright and 'chirpy'. Frequently heard is the 'song' of the male, given when advertising to the female from close to the nest, a series of chirps and cheeps slightly varying in pitch, such as "cheerp cheerp chilp chahp chaairp chearp…", or a more liquid "tchlrrp schleeip schlep tchleeip schleeip schlrrp..", etc. Other calls include a more clipped and drier "cheeup" or "chuurp", often repeated and given excitedly by a group, plus a disyllabic conversational "che'chep". It calls in flight with a single "cherp" note or disyllabic "churrip", and in anxiety or excitement gives a harder more rattling "chrr'rr'rr'rr'rr".

FEMALE

Chaffinch

Fringilla coelebs

Length: 14–16cm
Wingspan: 24.5–28.5cm

FEMALE

The Chaffinch is a very common bird across the region and is found in a variety of habitats, as well as being a common sight in many gardens. The male in particular is one of the more handsome members of the garden avifauna, and his bright and cheery song makes for a happy backdrop of sound. Indeed, it is very satisfying to hear the first songsters rattling away merrily at the end of the long winter months. It is rather long-tailed, compact and sparrow-sized, although slimmer and more elegant than a House Sparrow. The male is ruddy-pink from the throat and cheeks down to the belly, with a blue-grey crown, nape and shoulder, a chestnut-brown back and black wings boldly marked with double white wingbars, a plumage which is

brightest in spring, with colours duller and more subdued in winter. In all plumages it shows white or pale wingbars, white sides to the tail and a grey-green rump, features that are important for identification in the female particularly. She is much more demure, often looking nondescript, with a sepia-monochrome plumage, dull buffish-white underparts, a pale head and face, and a darker grey-brown crown and nape.

FEMALE

MALE

MALE

well as feeding on seed put out on open ground, but they always prefer a clear view of their surroundings and of any possible dangers. Although generally seed-eating, they will occasionally use peanut feeders. In Britain, breeding commences in April and May, with the nest located in a tree or tall bush. The female makes a neat deep cup of moss, lichen, grass and roots, bound together with spider webs and lined with feathers, with this construction usually built tightly into a branch fork. The female lays four or five eggs, and will do all the incubation, which lasts for 12–13 days. The nestlings are fed by both parents and leave the nest after 13–16 days.

The Chaffinch is one of the commonest birds in Britain, where it is resident, although numbers are supplemented in winter by migrants from northern Europe. It can be found in a variety of wooded habitats, both coniferous and deciduous, and these can include parks, orchards, gardens and farmland with hedgerows. During the winter months it also ranges onto arable fields and other open areas, usually adjacent to woodland, and where it can often be encountered in flocks mixed with other species. It is commonly found feeding on the ground, retreating to nearby trees when disturbed, only to drop down once more when the coast is clear. In a garden environment Chaffinches frequently use seed feeders and bird tables, as

It has a wide repertoire of calls, the most familiar one being a sharp repeated "pink" or "fink", a rather soft "hyupp", frequently heard from flying birds, a clear, upwards-inflected "hweet", and a short buzzing even-toned "hwwrrr" or "zhwrrr" note, rather reminiscent of the song of the Brambling. The Chaffinch's song is one of the more familiar sounds of spring, a loud, vigorous and slightly accelerating series of sweet but hard notes, descending in four tonal steps and ending in a trisyllabic flourish. It is usually unvarying in delivery and can sound almost rattle like, such as "chich-ich-ich-ich-ich-ich churr'rr'rr'rr'rr' cho'cho'cho'cho'cho chippit' churri'weeoo". It typically lasts 2.5–3 seconds, however variations are possible and it may sing with varying and out-of-sequence pitches. The song can be heard from February to July, and less frequently in the autumn.

Greenfinch

Carduelis chloris

Length: 14–16cm
Wingspan: 24.5–27.5cm

A common and familiar garden bird, often seen sitting prominently and singing, or engaging in bat-like display flights over the rooftops. It is a big-headed, plump and compact finch, readily recognized by the bright yellow wing panel formed by yellow edging to the primaries, plus a deep, thick whitish or pale pink bill. It also shows prominent blocks of yellow on the sides of the tail, which contrast with the remainder of the black tail and are most noticeable when seen in flight. The male is uniform light green, with a more yellow tone on the breast, and a brighter yellow-green rump. The upperparts are rather greyer, with a grey panel on the wing and grey head sides. The female is duller, brownish-green and faintly streaked on the mantle, and juveniles are brown and more streaked, with paler underparts.

A common resident in our region, with some immigration in winter by northern birds. A bird of the woodland edge, it favours taller trees in clearings, scrub, hedgerows, parks and gardens, but can also be found on arable fields and other open habitats, often feeding on the ground. The Greenfinch has become a very widespread and common feeder in gardens and this has probably insulated it against potential losses due to agricultural intensification. Its diet consists of large seeds, such as rose hips and cereal grain, and sunflower seeds are a particular favourite. Invertebrates such as insects are also taken, particularly for feeding to nestlings. Greenfinches regularly visit bird tables, and particularly seed feeders, favouring those with a small perch so that they can sit facing the feeder. Like House Sparrows, they are quite fussy about which seeds they eat, and where mixed seed is used they will often throw all the other seeds onto the ground so as to get to the black sunflower seeds. They can also be attracted to peanuts and fat balls, and will eat fruit where available.

Breeding commences in April or May, and the female builds a bulky cup of grasses, stems and moss, lined with hair, fine stems and feathers, the male accompanying her as she does so. The nest is usually in a bush or hedge, with four or five eggs laid and incubated by the female only, for 14–15 days. Both parents feed the nestlings a regurgitated mix, and the young fledge after 14–16 days. Greenfinches have two or three broods per season, and the female may lay again soon after the previous brood has fledged, leaving the male to feed the young while she incubates a new clutch.

A vocal bird, with a range of bright and bouncy calls. Typically heard are monosyllablic 'chips' and nasal sounds, such as an upward-slurred "ju'wee"

FEMALE

MALE

MALE

and higher-pitched "chwai'ii" or "pwai'ii" notes, which may act as alarm or anxiety notes. It also gives a single or repeated "chud", "jup" or "ju'jup", often given in flight, or extended into a slow trilling "chid'id'id'id'id'id'id" or "jup'up'up'up'up", plus a faster, more silvery trilling "tchrr'r'r'r'r'r'r'r'r". It has two song types: the first is a frequently heard, very nasal, drawn-out and downwards-inflected "djeeeeeuuuooo", lasting 1–1.6 seconds in length, with regular longer pauses between. A flatter or slightly upwards-inflected version of this is also given, as in "jweeeiiie", The more complex song incorporates many of these calls, including the "djeeuuuoo" sound, and alternates between Canary-like trills and other more slowly delivered notes, such as "djuw djuw djuw, jup jup jup, chi'di'di'di'di'dit, ju'wee, chud'chd'chd, chid'id'id 'id'id'id'id, ju'wee, djui djui djui djui, tilng tilng tilng tilng, tiisssrrrrrr, djeeeeeuuuooo...", etc. The song is often given in a bat-like display flight.

Goldfinch

Carduelis carduelis

Length: 12–13.5cm

Wingspan: 21–25.5cm

The Goldfinch is one of the most attractive birds likely to be seen in a garden. The head is white with a large red patch from the forehead around the face to the chin, and with a black crown and nape that curls downwards and forwards to the shoulder. The wings are black with a broad golden-yellow stripe across the flight feathers and greater coverts, and large white spots on the tips of the flight feathers, visible at rest. The underparts are white with buffy-brown flanks and

JUVENILE

an incomplete breast band. The mantle is brown, the rump is white and the forked tail is black with white spots. The sexes are rather similar, but on closer inspection males can be distinguished by a larger, darker red mask that extends just behind the eye; in females the mask falls short of the eye. The bill is long and pointed, ideal for teasing out small seeds. Juveniles are similar to adults except for having a plain head, a greyer back, and a brown-streaked breast. The collective noun for a group of Goldfinches is, appropriately enough, a 'charm'. Their population underwent a serious decline in the 1970s and 80s, probably as a result of the shift towards intensive agriculture, but they now seem to be thriving, particularly in and around gardens.

Resident across most of Britain and the Continent, although more easterly and northern populations move south in winter, outside the breeding season it can often be seen in flocks, feeding on weedy margins. It favours deciduous and mixed woodland edges, farmland hedgerows, orchards, parks, gardens and overgrown waste ground, frequently close to human habitation. The favoured diet consists of small seeds from plants such as thistles, teasels, daisies, dandelion, alder and birch, with the seeds often eaten when only half-ripe. Insects and other invertebrates are taken in summer, and especially for feeding nestlings. Goldfinches increasingly use garden bird feeders, favouring sunflower hearts, black sunflower seeds and peanuts, but most popular of all are nyger seeds, which can be provided for them in special nyger seed feeders. These are similar to a normal seed feeder but have very small holes,which prevent the tiny seeds from spilling out and also allow access only to thin-billed birds such as Goldfinches.

Breeding commences in April and May, and the female builds a cup-shaped nest of moss, grass and lichen, lined with wool and plant down. The nest is usually in a tree towards the end of a spreading branch, and four to six eggs are laid. Incubation is by the female for 13–15 days, and both parents feed the young until fledging takes place at 14–17 days. The young are dependent on the adults for at least one week after leaving the nest. There are two, and sometimes three, broods in a season.

A vocal bird with a variety of calls, the typical contact call being a cheery, variable "twiddit'widdit", also given in single "twtt" components or extended into "di'wit'iwit'iwidli'wit", when it sounds more like a segment of song. It also gives a slightly mewing and nasal "tch'weeoo", "theoo'wt" and "diu'lii", and a harsh buzzing "jhr'r'r'r'r'r" or "jjh'jjh'jjh'jit". The song, given from a perch and also in flight, is a bright, fast, tinkling, rattling and trilling sequence with a bell-like quality, as in "twiddli'widdli'twidi'trrrwiddit-ti'r'r'r'r'r'r'r'r-jjeeoow", sometimes given in a continuous sequence or in well-marked phrases of 2–3 seconds long, interspersed with pauses. Although quite complex and often variable, it is usually recognizable by the inclusion of call notes.

MALE

Bullfinch

Pyrrhula pyrrhula

Length: 15.5–17.5cm
Wingspan: 22–29cm

FEMALE

MALE

One of the most exotic-looking and attractive birds likely to be encountered in a garden, the Bullfinch has a plump and rounded body, a large head and a short, thick black bill. A black cap extends on to the face and around the bill, with a black tail contrasting with the white rump and black wings, plus a broad whitish wingbar on the tips of the greater coverts. The upperparts are grey, tinged browner in the female. The male has soft pinkish-red underparts from cheek to belly; on the female these are greyish-buff. Bullfinches are usually encountered sneaking along hedgerows, their white rumps a sure indicator as they flit discreetly from bush to bush, with their call often being the first indication of their presence. The nominate race or 'Northern Bullfinch', which occasionally occurs in Britain as a winter visitor, is larger than the resident British race, and the underparts of the male are a more intense rosy-pink, while the upperparts are paler.

Generally rather secretive, the Bullfinch favours deciduous and mixed woodland with dense undergrowth, as well as coniferous forest in the north of its range. It can be found along woodland edge, clearings, tall scrub, hedgerows, parks, large gardens, churchyards and seasonally

MALE

in orchards. It is resident in Britain, but has undergone a sharp fall in numbers in recent decades, with the loss of choice hedgerow and woodland edge habitat and the general intensification of agriculture. This decline followed a sharp increase in the 1950s, when Bullfinches caused problems to the fruit-growing industry, leading to widespread trapping in order to control their numbers. Their diet consists of the seeds of fleshy fruits such as cherries, and the buds of fruit trees. They also eat insects and feed their nestlings on invertebrates. In a garden they will also take seed from a hanging seed feeder, being particularly fond of sunflower hearts, and will also take suet cake.

Breeding commences in April or May, the female building a nest of twigs, moss and lichen, with a neat inner cup of roots and hair and located in a dense bush. Four to five eggs are laid and incubated solely by the female for 14–16 days, the male bringing food to her as she does so. The young are fed by both parents, the female sitting tight and brooding the hatchlings at first

while the male brings food. The young fledge after 15–17 days, and there are usually two broods. Unlike many other garden birds, breeding pairs of Bullfinch stay together throughout the year rather than separating after breeding.

The commonly heard call note is a piping single note, used as a contact call. It is a pleasant soft "peuw" or "heouw", slightly descending at the end and repeated at regular intervals. It can be quite far-carrying. Birds of the nominate race or 'Northern Bullfinch' have a different 'trumpeting' call, a higher-pitched "heeh" or "pihh", as well as a quiet "tip" note. The song, usually given by the male, is rarely heard, no doubt partly due to its being rather quiet and often only audible from close range. It is a rambling twittering without clear phrases, including typical call notes and some very nasal and deep double notes similar to the call, as well as long purring wheezes and higher-pitched long piping notes, such as "hong-hong tu'tu'tu'didi'peew heeuuuw pwrrrrrrr heeeeee hong-hong tu'di'tu'di'tuu hwrrrrrr…".

FEMALE

Bird Species/Where Seen:	Date:	Time:

Bird Species/Where Seen:	Date:	Time:

Bird Species/Where Seen:	Date:	Time:

Bird Species/Where Seen:	Date:	Time:

Artwork Credits

Brin Edwards
Blackbird p30b,31b
Black-headed Gull p10t
Blue Tit p34t
Bullfinch p54b,55
Carrion Crow p42t
Chaffinch p48t,49
Collared Dove p17
Dunnock p26t
Great Tit p36
Greenfinch p50
Green Woodpecker p20t,21
Goldfinch p53

House Martin p22t,23t
House Sparrow p46b,47
Jackdaw p40
Long-tailed Tit p33t
Robin p28t
Starling p44b
Woodpigeon p14b, 15
Wren p24b
Mike Langman
Blackbird p7,30t,31t
Black-headed Gull p10b,11
Blue Tit p34b,35
Bullfinch p54t

Carrion Crow & Hooded Crow
p42b,43
Chaffinch p48b
Collared Dove p16
Dunnock p26b,27
Great Tit p37
Greenfinch p51
Green Woodpecker p5,20b
Goldfinch p52
House Sparrow p46t
House Martin p4,22b,23b
Jackdaw p41
Long-tailed Tit p32,33b

Magpie p38,39
Pied Flycatcher p9
Robin p28b,29
Rock Dove & Feral Pigeons
p12,13
Starling p 44t,45
Spotted Flycatcher p6
Swift p18,19
Tawny Owl p2
Woodpigeon p14t
Wren p3,24t,25

This short book had been taken from
A Guide to the Garden Birds of Britain and Northern Europe by Dave Farrow
Originally published by Carlton Books in 2009
Text and artwork © 2020 Welbeck Non-fiction Limited